2019

FUNDAMENTALS OF REAL ESTATE INVESTING

WEALTH CREATION THROUGH REAL ESTATE INVESTING

ORLANDO MAIS FCCA, MSL, MST
OMAIS.FCCA@GMAIL.COM

Acknowledgement

This book is dedicated to my wife Dania Mais whose support and encouragement has been a source of inspiration for completing this project. To my children Nicholas, Kiera and Kristina who have always supported me throughout the process of authoring this book.

Contents

Fundamentals of Real Estate Investing

What is real estate?

Real estate is property made up of land as well as anything on it, including buildings, animals, and natural resources. There are two primary classes of real estate namely commercial and residential real estate.

Commercial Real Estate

Commercial real estate (CRE) is property, used solely for business purposes and often leased to tenants for that purpose. This property category further divides into four classes that include office, industrial, multifamily, and retail.

Residential Rental Property

Residential rental property is a type of investment property that derives more than 80% of its revenue from dwelling units. Real estate investing is one of the fastest ways to build wealth. Whether you are new to real estate investing or a seasoned investor, if done properly you can create a strong and stable financial future, however there are certain steps that you must take to ensure success.

Important Considerations before Investing

The most important thing for any real estate investor is to learn as much as possible about the market and key concepts involved in real estate investing. Develop your ability to spot opportunities before others do and act decisively.

Be sure to properly analyze any deal before you sign any contracts with sellers. Inform yourself on how to calculate certain key financial metrics such as net return on investment (ROI), carrying costs, mortgage payments, interest costs, depreciation, etc.

You do not have to be an expert just inform yourself and factor in these key financial metrics before deciding. Seek the assistance of a friend or a professional if you are unsure how to proceed.

Just ensure that at the end of the day the investment will generate positive cash flow as you will need cash to pay your mortgage and other cost involved with owning the property.

Devise a plan and adopt a long-term perspective. Wealth creation does not happen overnight. Start small but think big. Begin with one rental unit and set a goal to add at least one property per year. This is possible if you keep your deals cash flow positive, take advantage of the appreciation in value of the properties you own and utilize smart financing options.

Avoid buying condominiums for use as rental property as you will have difficulty leveraging equity in obtaining financing due to banks aversion to financing condominiums. Banks are unwilling to finance these types of properties for retail investors due to cumbersome condominium rules, past problems with delinquent condominium owners, and lack of adequate insurance by some condominiums.

In addition to the negatives outlined above, condominium fees have a huge negative effect on cashflow from units. Not to mention the difficulty you face in qualifying tenants with the condominium board. Condominium may appear to be a cheap way to get started in real estate rental, but the issues you will face are not worth the effort.

Another key consideration you need to pay attention to before you decide on selecting a rental property is the location of property. This is because you will need your property to be in an area that will provide you with a reasonable assurance that you will be able to find good tenants and minimize issues with property vacancy. You cannot generate positive cashflow if the property sits vacant. Property that are close to places of employment or schools are always in great demand.

Valuation Methods

In buying real estate you will need to obtain an appraisal report from a licensed property appraiser. This is essential for establishing the value of the property being considered. Financial institutions and private lenders rely of these reports to determine the viability of loans used to finance the purchase. Appraisers use several different approaches to determine the value of the property depending on the type of property being evaluated.

According to the FDIC all federally related transactions that are commercial real estate transactions having a transaction value of more than $500,000 shall require an appraisal prepared by a State certified appraiser. The institution may engage a certified appraiser to complete the appraisal.

It is important to familiarize yourself with the different valuation methods by appraisers so that you can perform quick estimates to gauge the potential of any real estate investment being contemplated. The most common valuation methods are sales comparison, cost approach, and income capitalization approach.

Sales Comparison Approach

This method analyzes the recent sales price of comparable properties and is mostly used in valuing land and residential real estate, especially single-family homes. Properties are only considered comparable if they are like the property and have been sold within the year under ordinary market conditions. Other factors such as square footage, number of bedrooms and number of bathrooms also affect the valuation.

Cost Approach

The concept of the cost approach is stems from the principle of not more for a rental property than the cost to construct that unit. It uses the sales comparison approach to determine the underlying value of the land then taking depreciation into account estimate the costs of building the property.

This method is typically used for properties that are constructed and not sold such as schools, religious institutions, government buildings, and hospitals. Once the property's land value is estimated, it is added to the estimated building costs which can be determined by multiplying the cost per square to the total square footage of the comparable units.

Income Capitalization Approach

This method is used for all income properties such as apartment buildings, commercial real estate, and multifamily homes. The income capitalization approach considers the return on investment and the net income of a property.

It is subdivided into two property valuation methods 1) direct capitalization and 2) gross income multipliers.

Direct capitalization estimates the effective gross income by considering the impact of vacancies then subtracts operating expenses to calculate the net operating income. The property's value is then estimated using the property's capitalization rate, or cap rate, and net operating income.

The gross income multipliers approach is used for income earning properties that were not originally intended to be rental properties for example homes used for residence. The gross income of the property is calculated and is used to divide the sales price of the property in determining the gross income multiplier, which is then used to find the property's market value.

How Wealth is Created in Real Estate

In real estate wealth is created in two primary ways, one is through the is through the appreciation in value of the property and the second through buildup of passive income generated from free cash flow produced by renting the property.

Property appreciation is the increase in value of real estate over time due to an increase in demand or changes made to the property by the investor such as adding a bedroom or bathroom. In addition, property value is adjusted to reflect a change in inflation making real estate a good store of value in times of high inflation.

Real estate rental is a wonderful way to generate free cash flow however a disciplined approach is required to succeed at this. Cash flow is the lifeblood of any business, for any business to succeed it needs to be able to generate positive free cash flow.

The single most important concept that you need to understand for building wealth through passive income earned in real estate investing is the concept of positive free cash flow. Since real estate investing is a cash-intensive business that normally requires a lot of upfront capital you will need to obtain financing for your project. When considering financing deals, you need to determine whether they will generate positive free cash flow.

In a nutshell positive cash flow simply means that the monthly income you receive from your property should exceed the amount you spend on expenses maintaining that property.

This means that rent collected from your tenants should cover your mortgage, insurance, property taxes, and any other monthly, quarterly, or annual charges.

Leverage the Money of Others

Real estate allows investors to earn substantially higher returns of capital invested by using the money provided by banks, real estate syndication, real estate crowdfunding, or even owner financing, and other real estate investors. For example, a typical mortgage loan for an income property is about 80% as a 20% down payment is normally required.

If the real estate property is priced at $100,000, the investor will need a cash down payment of $20,000 cash investment from the real estate investor. Assume that the property is sold right away for $110,000, the profit would be ($110,000 – 100,000) $10,000. The real estate investor would have essentially made a 50% return on the cash investment. Having paid a full cash investment of $100,000 and selling for the same price would amount to a 10% return on investment only! See the illustration below:

	No Leverage	Leverage
Cost of Property	100,000	100,000
Investor Cash used in Financing	100,000	20,000
Bank Financing Used	0.00	80,000
Sale Price	110,000	110,000
Profit of sale	10,000	10,000
Rate of Return (Profit/Investment)	10%	50%

Tax-Free Cash Flow

Cash in the form of rent earned from real estate can result in tax-free cash flow unlike cash earned from other forms of investment such as interest or dividends.

Real estate investors who own rental properties can claim tax deductions such as: depreciation of an income property, interest on financing for rental properties, expenses relating to investment property repairs, local and long-distance travel, home office, employees for a real estate business, insurance for an investment property, professional and legal services

Real estate investors also have the option to avoid capital gains tax when selling an investment property through the 1031 tax exchange. As a result, the cash flow generated by the property can be used to pay down the mortgage or go towards enhancing the property and build long term equity for the investor.

Mistakes to Avoid

There are many common mistakes made by real estate investors that can have a detrimental effect on your plan for wealth creation. The good news is that there are ways to avoid making these mistakes. Before venturing into real estate investing you should become familiar with some of the common mistakes and devise a plan to avoid them.

Many investors get excited or carried away during the bidding process and end up overbidding on the project. Avoid this mistake because overpaying is a sure way to eat up any potential profits in a deal. In addition, it inflates your finance charges and restricts your flexibility in exiting or the property for a long time.

Never purchase investment properties without having title search performed by title company or an attorney and always obtain adequate title insurance. This may seem obvious, but it is important that it should not be overlooked.

Avoid getting in deals where there are contingency clause surrounding the title insurance. This occurs sometimes where foreclosed properties are sold at auction. Often there are outstanding liens with a city or county that may run into thousands of dollars and you may be left the headache of resolving those issues.

Make sure to keep renovations within reason. Do not make lavish improvements to your investment properties. Improvements should be targeted and should not be substantially greater than the comparative properties in the area your property is located.

Be sure to research the rating or obtain referrals for any contractors used in renovating your projects. This is because there are many dishonest individuals waiting to take advantage of an inexperienced investor. Hiring the wrong people can create major headaches for you.

Disputes with a contractor will tie-up your project and may result in a contractor's lien on your property that you will need to address in a timely manner. Ensure that estimates for work to be done are documented in enough details outlining the nature and extent of work to be done. Be sure to align your expectations of the work to be performed with what is documented in the agreement with the contractor.

Do not invest without carrying out adequate research into the property, the location, schools, employment opportunities, crime rate, property values of similar units, vacancy rates in the area, utilities available etc.

Leave room in your budget for unexpected events such as a vacancy or unexpected repairs required. Do no overextend yourself or make any significant financial commitments for a few months after closing on your property. Create a cash reserve to cover carrying cost for a few months.

Options Available to Potential Investors

There are various avenues for a potential real estate investor depending on the amount of money you intend to allocate to your real estate portfolio.

You may invest directly by purchasing and managing rental properties. This is the traditional approach used by many real estate investors. The objective is to build a portfolio of properties generating positive cash flow and leveraging equity buildup along with surplus cash to extend the portfolio.

Investors may purchase real properties with the intention to fix up and resell properties. These properties are not acquired for their rental income potential rather they are acquired because the investor believe they can unlock significant short-term value by renovating them.

Invest in real estate investment trusts (REITs). REITs allow investors to earn passive income in real estate without owning and managing the physical real estate. This is the cheapest and most accessible option oven to investors of all ages.

Another source of rental income may be derived by renting out a room in your primary residence.

Investors may participate in an online real estate platform that has a team in place to select, finance, and manage real estate. They may also participate through real estate wholesaling a process of finding deals and marketing them to buyers. Here the investor acts as a middleman and is not looking to take ownership of the property.

Purchasing and Managing Rental Properties

If you are new to real estate investing, I suggest you start small and gain an understanding of the business. This can be accomplished by researching cheaper units or pooling resources with a friend or family member who is willing to share the risks and rewards of the venture.

In choosing rental property the goal should not be buying the most expensive property in the best part of town. The focus should be on the property that can provide the most income per dollar invested.

For example if a two bedroom room unit can only rent for $900 per month and you have two projects to choose from (one selling for $50,000 and the other in a nicer part of town selling for $100'000) all things equal, you should go with the cheaper unit if your goal is to build passive rental income. This is because your monthly carrying cost (i.e. mortgage, insurance, and property taxes) will be lower on the cheaper unit.

	Property A	Property B
Total Acquisition Cost	$50,000	$100,000
Monthly Finance charge at 6% (interest only)	$250	$500
Property Tax at 2%	$83	$167
Estimated Mortgage Insurance	$150	$300
Total Estimated Monthly Expenses	$483	$967
Rental Income	$900	$900
Free Cash Flow	$417	($67)

Although this is an oversimplified example it demonstrates the point that acquiring a cheaper property will be more beneficial to an investor wishing to build passive income and wealth through real estate.

If possible, your first property should be a multifamily unit such as a duplex or triplex. You may use one unit for your personal use and have the other unit cover your carrying cost or rent both unit and boost your cash flow from the property.

Fix and Flip

If your objective is to acquire real estate with the intention to sell for a short-term profit you will need to be aware of a couple of things.

You will also need to familiarize yourself with the property values in your area to estimate the As-is and After-repair values of the property. The As-is value is the value of the property without any repairs. After-repair value is as suggested, the value after you carry out any required repairs.

These are estimates only, but they will assist you in determining if the property is a worthwhile investment or if you will be able to handle the cost of repairs along with your other obligations after acquiring the property.

You will need to have a reliable team in place to assist with finding, contracting, financing, and renovating the intended property.

Particular attention to the desirability of the location is required to ensure the holding period is no longer than what is required to renovate and market the property.

In selecting a property for potential flips make sure to have a professional examine it before making an offer. Some cosmetic remodeling is normal when you buy a new investment property, however, try to avoid property requiring substantial repairs. Watch out for properties with unsound structures, substantial damage to or outdated plumbing, permit issues, substantial outstanding liens etc.

Older properties are notorious for having environmental hazards such as lead-based paint, asbestos, and radon gas. All these hazards are expensive to fix and will quickly eliminate any potential profit from your flip.

Make sure to ask specific questions pertaining the condition of the property. Try avoiding questions that will result in a simply yes or no answer. For example, you may as the following questions:

* When was the last time the roof was repaired?
* When was the last time the kitchen and bathroom were updated or improved?
* How long has the plumbing been in place and what types of pipes were used?
* What is the condition of the heating or cooling system or when were they last updated or replaced?

Getting the answer to these questions can save you a lot of time and money since they may enable you decide to terminate negotiations depending on the extent of work required to bring the property in line with current standards.

Real Estate Investment Trusts (REITs)

According to reit.com, a real estate investment trust ("REIT") is a company that owns, operates, or finances income-producing real estate. REITs provide all investors the chance to own valuable real estate, present the opportunity to access dividend-based income and total returns, and help communities grow, thrive, and revitalize.

The idea of REITS was conceived in the 1960s to facilitate the participation of the of a broader base of investors in the commercial real estate market. They enable the pooling of resources to finance income earning real estate assets and provide an income stream to their shareholders.

They are essentially the most accessible option for your average retail investor to add real estate to their portfolio. Retail investors may acquire shares in REITs through their stockbrokers or 401k funds. REITs are traded on major exchanges like stocks and they invest in real estate directly, either through properties or through mortgage investment.

Investors may acquire shares of individual companies, mutual funds made up of REITS, or exchange traded funds (ETFs) specializing in REITS. As a stockholder of a REIT you will earn a share of the income generated from its real estate investment and not having to worry about acquiring and managing rental properties.

In total, REITs of all types collectively own more than $3 trillion in gross assets across the U.S., with stock-exchange listed REITs owning approximately $2 trillion in assets, representing more than 500,000 properties. U.S. listed REITs have an equity market capitalization of more than $1 trillion (reit.com).

Equity REITs are divided into sub-industries namely retail, industrial, diversified, hotel & resort, office, residential, and specialized. They will invest in one area of real estate or in one geographic location. Because they offer investors a high-dividend distribution, REITs receive special tax considerations from the IRS and are considered industry experts as a very liquid method of investing in real estate.

According to Investopedia.com REITs provide one of the lowest starting capital cost options for getting into the asset class. Several major REITs offer dividend reinvestment plans (DRIPs). These plans can provide access to commercial real estate for as little as the cost of one share of stock with little in the way of fees. Likewise, almost every major mutual fund company offers a REIT focused option. Many of these come with low starting investments between $500 and $2,500.

The IRS provides guidelines required to be met for the qualification of a REIT. To qualify as a REIT a company must:

1. Invest at least 75% of its total assets in real estate

2. Derive at least 75% of its gross income from rents from real property, interest on mortgages financing real property or from sales of real estate.

3. Pay at least 90% of its taxable income in the form of shareholder dividends each year.

4. Be an entity that is taxable as a corporation.

5. Be managed by a board of directors or trustees.

6. Have a minimum of 100 shareholders.

7. Have no more than 50% of its shares held by five or fewer individuals.

Since REITs must pay out 90% of taxable income as a cash dividend to shareholders, this makes an investment in REITs a reliable source of cashflow. The only issue is that with such a high payout ratio there is very little income remaining for reinvestment in the REIT as a result the ability for capital appreciation is limited to the growth in the value of the share price of the REIT stock.

Real Estate Wholesaling

For the knowledgeable investor real estate wholesaling is an effective way to benefit from unearthing value in real estate without using any of your money. Wholesaling is ideal for someone with little or no money to use for the 20% down payment required for investment properties and it does not require a license.

However, it does require a knowledge of the local real estate market, a strategy for locating deals, excellent negotiating skills, an effective marketing strategy, and effective communication skills.

Real estate wholesaling involves identifying real estate deals, negotiating contracts with sellers, identifying potential buyers, and assigning your rights to purchase the property to one of the potential buyers identified.

The wholesaler does not intend to acquire title to the property or to carry out any repairs before reselling. The objective is to sell the property before title is transferred to the wholesaler or before the contract with the seller of the property closes.

Once the wholesaler identifies a potential property and enters a contract the property is then marketed to identify potential buyers. The wholesaler will market the property at a higher price than his contracted price with the original seller. Because of this they need to be good at negotiating since the wholesaler will have to negotiate with the property seller (when putting the property under contract) as well as the property buyer (when selling the property).

To limit the wholesaler's risk, it is important for the wholesaler to have an escape clause included in the contract with the seller of the property in the event they are unable to find a buyer before expected closing date.

About the Author

Orlando Mais is a Chartered Accountant, business consultant, serial entrepreneur and author who has several startups and conducted multiple real estate transactions. He holds a master's degree in Business Management and Leadership and a Master of Science degree in Taxation. He is a fellow member of the Association of Certified Chartered Accountants (ACCA), a global accounting body head quartered in London, UK. He lives in Florida with his wife and their three resourceful children.

www.ingramcontent.com/pod-product-compliance
Lightning Source LLC
Chambersburg PA
CBHW051123250726
48655CB00007B/2857